A DISCOVERY BOOK

Robert Fulton

Steamboat Builder

by Joanne Landers Henry

illustrated by Tran Mawicke

GARRARD PUBLISHING COMPANY
CHAMPAIGN, ILLINOIS

To the memory of Walter D. Henry

The Discovery Books are prepared
under the educational supervision of

Mary C. Austin, Ed.D.
Professor of Education
University of Hawaii
Honolulu

Library of Congress Cataloging in Publication Data

Henry, Joanne Landers.
   Robert Fulton, steamboat builder.

   (Discovery books)
   SUMMARY: A brief biography of the portrait painter
and inventor of the submarine and steamboat.

   1. Fulton, Robert, 1765-1815—Juvenile literature.
2. Steamboats—History—Juvenile literature.
[1. Fulton, Robert, 1765-1815. 2. Steamboats—
History. 3. Inventors] I. Mawicke, Tran, illus.
II. Title.

VM140.F9H4   623.82′4′0924 [B] [92]   74–18326
ISBN 0–8116–6317–5

2064345

Contents

Chapter 1

The Gift

The schoolroom was quiet. Only the *scratch-scratch* of the children's goose-quill pens could be heard.

Everyone in the one-room school except Robert Fulton was busy writing. Schoolwork bored nine-year-old Robert. He was working on something he thought more important.

He sat hunched over his desk. His brown curly hair fell forward as he worked. With a hand and arm he hid his secret from the schoolmaster's sharp eyes.

"Let me see," John Finley whispered

in Robert's ear. The two boys sat together at a rough board desk.

Suddenly a shadow fell across the desk. "What mischief is this, Master Fulton?" schoolmaster Caleb Johnson asked. He picked up the copybook that lay open in front of Robert.

On one page Robert had practiced writing. On the other page he had painted a picture of a pretty, gray, two-story stone house. Beside it were gently rolling fields colored yellow-gold and brown.

"Please, sir," Robert answered. "I was trying out John's new paints. It's a picture of the house where I was born."

"A waste of valuable paper!" the schoolmaster scolded. "You never work at what you should. I fear, Master Fulton, that you are a dull boy."

6

Robert felt angry and hurt. Tears came into his dark eyes.

John saw how unhappy Robert was. After school he gave his paints to Robert. "You take the paints," he said. "You paint much better than I ever will. You could be a real artist someday."

Robert was very pleased with the gift. He had never owned paints like these. He had always painted pictures with colors made from the juices of berries and other plants.

Robert wanted to do something nice for John. Suddenly he had an idea. He would make a very special gift for his friend.

With a happy heart, he rushed out of the schoolyard. He hurried past the printer's shop, then the shoemaker's and the blacksmith's.

At last he came to a gunsmith's shop. Like most of the houses and shops in Lancaster, Pennsylvania, it was made of brick and stone.

The gunsmith made both guns and bullets. He made the bullets from lead. Robert asked if he could have some of the lead scraps.

Next he went to Nicholas Miller's cabinet shop. Mr. Miller made tables, chairs, beds, and other furniture. Robert asked him for a thin, narrow piece of wood. He asked if he could use Mr. Miller's tools.

Mr. Miller liked Robert. He said yes.

With a wooden hammer, Robert pounded the soft lead. He shaped it until it was round and thin and about five inches long.

With a knife he split the soft wood into two narrow pieces. He hollowed out one of the pieces. Then he placed the round lead in it. He glued the other piece of wood to the first one, to hold the lead in place. The lead was longer than its thin wooden case.

Now, Robert wondered, would it work? Carefully he drew the letters *R* and *F* in dark, heavy lines.

"Hurrah!" he shouted. His homemade pencil wrote, just as he hoped it would.

Excited, he hurried home to show his mother.

"Your head is full of good ideas, Robert." She smiled. "I believe you could make almost anything. If your father were alive now, he would be proud of you."

Mr. Fulton had died when Robert was very young. He had been a tailor. Then he had decided to become a farmer. He had bought a large farm in Little Britain Township. The farm was not far from Lancaster. It was here that Robert was born on November 14, 1765.

Mr. Fulton was not a very good farmer, so the family soon moved back to Lancaster. Although he never made much money, Mr. Fulton became one of the town's leading citizens.

After Mr. Fulton died, Robert's mother had to make every penny count. There were the shopkeepers and the schoolmaster to pay. There were five children to feed and clothe.

Later Robert showed the pencil to his brother and sisters. Mary and Abraham, who were younger than Robert, drew pictures with it. His two older sisters, Peggy and Belle, tried it too.

The next day Robert took the pencil to school. John was happily surprised with the gift. The other children crowded around to see it.

Suddenly the schoolmaster appeared. "What's this, Master Fulton, more mischief?"

"No, sir," Robert answered. "It's a pencil. I made it for John."

The schoolmaster looked closely at the pencil. "Why, you've done a very good job indeed!" he said. "It would cost a lot to buy one in a shop." Then he nodded his head. "Perhaps, Master Fulton, you are not such a dull boy after all."

Chapter *2*

Sign Painter

Eleven-year-old Robert watched as American soldiers marched through the streets. He saw long lines of captured British soldiers led into town. Supply wagons loaded high with clothing, blankets, and guns rattled by.

More than a year had passed since the colonists in America had declared their independence. But the king of England would not give up the colonies. He said that they still belonged to England.

So the thirteen colonies joined together to fight for their freedom. Pennsylvania was one of those colonies. Lancaster, Pennsylvania, where Robert lived, was an important supply center for the colonial soldiers.

To Robert, this fall of 1777 was an exciting time. He was curious about everything that went on in the town. He was especially curious about how the soldiers' rifles were made. Many of them came from the gunsmiths' shops in Lancaster.

One day Robert went to Mr. Isch's gunsmith shop. He was sure Mr. Isch would welcome him. Mr. Isch had known Robert's father.

Inside the large workshop, Robert watched as the men worked. He asked them many questions.

Then he saw Mr. Isch. He went

toward the shop owner. "May I see the rifle you are working on, sir?" Robert asked.

With a smile Mr. Isch handed the rifle to Robert.

Robert ran his fingers over the finely carved designs on its wooden shoulder piece. Mr. Isch explained that this rifle had been specially ordered by a rich gentleman.

"Now, because of the war, most of my guns are not so fancy as this one," Mr. Isch went on. "It takes too long to put designs on them."

Robert enjoyed his visit. He asked Mr. Isch if he could come to the shop again.

"You are always welcome in my shop," Mr. Isch answered.

After this, Robert visited the shop whenever he could. Sometimes the workmen showed him how to run their machines and use their tools. Robert was quick to learn, and he easily made friends with the men.

"He is a handy lad to have around," one of the workmen told Mr. Isch. "He knows almost as much about machines and tools as we do."

One day Robert stopped in to show Mr. Isch a drawing he had made. It was a design for a rifle's wooden shoulder piece. Robert had worked out many different designs, but he liked this one the best.

"It's very good!" Mr. Isch said, surprised. "I would like to use it for one of my special rifles."

"Sir, I can make as many designs as you want," Robert said quickly. "There are a lot of things I could do around the shop. May I come to work here?"

Times were hard and money was scarce. Robert felt he was old enough to work a few hours each day after school. No matter how little he earned, it would be a great help to his mother.

Mr. Isch smiled. "When you are a few years older, we will talk about a job. But for now, work at your art, Robert. It will be useful to you someday."

Someday was not soon enough. After Robert left Mr. Isch's, he walked down the street lined with shops. He was looking for another place where he might find a job.

Each shop had a sign hanging outside. Many had large pictures painted on them. The pictures showed what the shops sold. Some of the signs were old and faded.

Suddenly Robert had an idea. He

went into one shop after another. He asked each shopkeeper if he would like to have his sign repainted.

At first only a few shopkeepers said yes. Later, others saw Robert's work and liked it. Soon he was able to earn a little money each week.

"Benjamin West painted signs, too, when he was young," Mrs. Fulton told Robert.

Over the years, Robert had heard many stories about Benjamin West. Now he was a very famous artist. He had been born in Pennsylvania. Before Robert was born, Mr. West had painted small portraits of Mr. and Mrs. Fulton.

Robert looked at the two portraits. Someday, he dreamed, he might be a famous artist like Mr. West.

Chapter 3

A Special Celebration

On July 4, 1777, Lancaster had celebrated the first birthday of the Declaration of Independence.

That night hundreds of candles had twinkled brightly from all of the house and shop windows in the town. Robert thought it was one of the most beautiful sights he had ever seen.

All through the following year he saved the ends of used candles for the next celebration. Robert planned to melt the small pieces and make large candles from them. He hoped to have one for every window of the house.

On the first day of July 1778, the town council put a notice outside the courthouse. The notice said that no candles could be burned for the celebration this year. The colonists were still fighting the revolutionary war. Food, clothing, blankets, and candles were needed by the soldiers. The townspeople must use carefully what they had.

Sadly Robert told his family the news.

"Can't you think of another way to celebrate?" his brother Abraham asked.

Robert shook his head, but he promised to try.

A few days later he thought of an idea. He would make this year's celebration one his brother and sisters would never forget.

At first Robert wondered if his idea would work. He found a book to help him, and he studied it carefully. Then Robert drew plans on a piece of paper.

He studied his drawings. "Yes," he said to himself, "I'm sure it will work."

He took all the candle ends he had saved to a shopkeeper. He traded them for some gunpowder.

"I know you are a careful lad, Robert Fulton," the shopkeeper said. "So I will give you the gunpowder. But what are you going to do with it?"

Robert told his friend what he was going to make.

The shopkeeper laughed. "I'll believe it when I see it, young Master Fulton."

"Then come to the town square tomorrow night," Robert said with a smile.

He went to another shop. There,

with some pennies he had saved, he bought several large sheets of very stiff, heavy paper.

The shopkeeper was curious. He wanted to know what Robert was going to make. Robert told him.

The shopkeeper smiled and shook his head. "That's impossible!"

"No, sir," Robert answered happily. "There is nothing that is impossible."

The news that Robert was planning a celebration spread quickly among the townspeople. By sunset on the Fourth of July, a large crowd had gathered at the town square.

When Robert arrived, he was carrying a handful of tubes made from the stiff paper.

"What are you going to do with those?" Abraham wanted to know. "I saw you put gunpowder in them."

Robert smiled. "Just you wait and see." In a few minutes he was ready to begin.

One by one he set off his homemade rockets. They shot into the air with a bang and lighted the sky as they burned.

A cheer went up from the crowd. Robert's family and friends crowded around him.

"This was a great Fourth of July!" his brother shouted happily. Robert's sisters and mother agreed.

"Next time young Fulton says he can do a thing, I'll believe him," one shopkeeper said to another.

Chapter 4

Paddle Wheels

Thirteen-year-old Robert put his pole down into the water. He pushed with all his strength. Slowly the small flat-bottomed boat moved forward. Then his friend, Chris Gumpf, put his pole into the water and pushed.

All morning the boys struggled against the swift current of the Conestoga Creek. Poling the clumsy boat was hard work.

"By the time we get upstream, we

won't have enough strength left to pull in a fish," Robert said, stopping for a moment to catch his breath.

"We need something to push the boat for us," Chris said. "Maybe we could make something."

Suddenly Robert remembered the story about William Henry's steamboat. Mr. Henry, who lived in Lancaster, had once built a boat with a steam engine in it. At the rear of the boat he had put a large paddle wheel. This wheel, turned by the engine, made the boat go.

"What are you thinking about?" Chris asked.

"Mr. Henry's boat," Robert answered. "He used a steam engine to make his boat go."

"Yes, but his boat sank," Chris said. "Besides, even the smallest steam engine would be too big for this little boat."

"I know," Robert agreed. "But I'll think of something practical that will work on your boat."

A few days later, Robert went for a short visit to his aunt's. She lived on a farm not far from Lancaster. She needed him to help with some farm work.

Robert found farm life dull and much too quiet. He missed the excitement of Lancaster.

To make the time pass more quickly, he began to think about Chris's boat. How could he make it go so he and Chris would not have to work so hard? He thought again of Mr. Henry's boat.

"Paddle . . . *paddle* wheels!" he said to himself. He would build paddle wheels for the boat. Somehow he would have to find a way to turn them by hand.

"I'll build a model first," he decided. "I'll make it look just like the flat-bottomed boat. Then I can try my invention out, to see if it will really work."

He spent every spare hour working on the model. When it was finished, he showed it to his aunt.

"These are paddle wheels," he told her. He pointed to the large wheels on each side, set near the middle of the boat.

"The paddles are fastened to the wheels," he went on. "They dip down into the water like oars and push the boat along."

Robert's aunt was amazed. "But, Robert," she wanted to know, "what will make these paddle wheels of yours go around?"

He showed her a handle inside the boat. It was shaped like a square letter *U*, and it was attached to each wheel.

"You see," he said, "when I turn this handle, it makes the paddle wheels go around and around."

The next day Robert returned to Lancaster. He had to leave the model with his aunt. It was too big to carry on the long walk home.

As soon as he could, Robert told Chris about the model boat he had built. Chris was eager to try out Robert's invention. So the boys set to work to make paddle wheels for the real boat.

Other boys heard that Robert and Chris were building something strange.

They came down to the creek to watch. One laughed and made jokes about the paddle wheels.

Chris became very angry. He wanted to hit the boy in the nose.

"We can't stop work now, Chris," Robert said calmly. "Here, give me a hand with these wheels."

Chris helped Robert put the wheels on the boat. Then the boys pushed it away from shore.

Robert stood in the center of the boat ready to turn the crank. Chris sat in the rear. There they had added a rudder.

"We'll need the rudder to steer with," Robert had told Chris.

The boat drifted toward the middle of the creek. Robert slowly began to turn the crank.

Splash-splash, splash-splash went the

paddle wheels as the paddles dipped in and out of the water.

Chris guided the boat upstream. Robert turned the crank faster and faster. Little by little the boat gained speed.

"Robert, it works—it works!" Chris cried.

There was a shout from the boys on shore. "Look at them go!"

Robert smiled. He felt happy. His invention really was practical.

Chapter 5

Philadelphia Artist

The early morning November air was sharp and cold. The horses had been hitched up, and the stagecoach was ready to go. Several passengers had already climbed aboard.

Robert's clothes and paintbrushes had been tied into a neat bundle. He put it under one of the stage's rough wooden seats.

Mrs. Fulton looked up proudly at her tall, slim, good-looking son. "You seem older than your seventeen years,

Robert. Yet I will still worry about you. Philadelphia is a very big city."

Robert put his arm around his mother's shoulders. "There is nothing to worry about," he said. "I have work waiting for me." 2064345

One of his grown-up friends had found a job for Robert in Philadelphia. It was with a silversmith who made jewelry.

"Philadelphia is a city of great opportunity," Robert said cheerfully. "I am lucky to have a job there."

Mrs. Fulton smiled and nodded her head. She knew that Robert was right to take the job. He had worked for a gunsmith during the last years of the war. But finally the fighting had ended. The colonists had won their independence from England. Now there would be little work for Lancaster's many gunsmiths.

Robert gave his mother another hug. Then he climbed aboard the coach.

As it rattled and bumped over the dirt road, Robert thought about the exciting days ahead. There would be much to learn from the silversmith. Perhaps, too, he could learn more about drawing and painting. He still dreamed of someday becoming an artist.

After many long hours of travel, Robert at last arrived in Philadelphia. Eagerly he set out to explore the city.

He was so interested in all he saw that he forgot about time. Then it started to get dark. He knew that he must find the silversmith's, so he hurried on his way. Tomorrow would be the first day of a great new adventure.

In the weeks that followed, Robert helped the smith make beautiful jewelry. There were necklaces, belt buckles, and other lovely pieces to work on. It was almost like being an artist, he told himself.

When he had time off, he visited an art collection. During the next year, he copied many of the pictures he saw there. This, he knew, was a good way to learn how to draw and paint.

One day he showed some of his best pictures to the silversmith. Most were small copies of portraits he had seen in the art collection.

"These look very good to me," the smith said. "I think I can also use your talents as a painter."

Robert could not imagine what the smith had in mind. But he would surely like to spend more time painting. A few days later, the smith asked Robert to paint a tiny picture. A wealthy woman wanted a miniature portrait of herself done quickly. The smith would make a fancy silver frame for it.

The next day the woman came to the shop. She sat while Robert made a careful drawing of her head and shoulders. She would not have to pose for him while he worked on the painting itself. He would paint the colors from memory.

A week later the woman came for the finished picture and frame. She was very pleased with them.

"Your painting, Master Fulton, makes me look prettier than I really am," she told Robert.

"Indeed, no, madam!" Robert said with a charming smile.

The lady liked Robert's work and his good manners. She told all her friends about the new young artist.

Soon many of them came to the

silversmith's. They wanted Robert to paint miniature portraits of them too. Robert spent more and more time painting. He earned extra money this way. Whenever he could, he sent some home to his mother.

At last he decided to open an artist's shop of his own. By now many people in Philadelphia knew that he painted. He had made many new friends too. He knew they would come to his shop and send others.

In 1785 he rented a shop at the corner of Second and Walnut streets. He hung a sign over the door. It read: "Robert Fulton, Miniature Painter."

He wished his mother were here to see his shop. How proud she would be!

Chapter 6

A Long Voyage

Robert could hardly believe he was here, in Benjamin Franklin's home. Why, he wondered, had the great Mr. Franklin sent for him?

Robert knew Mr. Franklin was one of the country's leaders. Most of Mr. Franklin's long life had been spent serving his country. He had worked hard for its independence. He was also famous as an inventor and an author.

"So you are the young artist I've heard so much about," Mr. Franklin said in a kindly tone. "I wonder if you would have time to do a large portrait of an old man like me?"

Robert smiled. "Indeed I would, sir. This will be the most important job I've had yet."

Mr. Franklin nodded. "When can we begin?"

"The first thing tomorrow morning," Robert said eagerly.

Mr. Franklin posed for Robert several hours a day. While Robert worked on the portrait, the two men talked. Sometimes they talked about inventions and new machines.

Robert still liked to draw plans for machines. He often worked on them in his spare time. He showed some of his sketches to Mr. Franklin.

"I hope you can paint my portrait as well as you draw plans for machines," Mr. Franklin joked.

"I'll do my best," Robert said with a smile.

When the painting was finished, Mr. Franklin said that he was very pleased with it.

Robert told Mr. Franklin he dreamed of being a great artist someday.

"Then you should go to London, England," Mr. Franklin said. "There you could study with a great artist. One of the finest teachers there is Benjamin West."

"When I was a boy I dreamed of being famous like Mr. West," Robert said excitedly. "I would rather study with him than with anyone else in the world."

He told Mr. Franklin that his parents had met Mr. West. "That was before I was born," Robert added. "He would not know me."

"I will write to Mr. West when you are ready to go," Mr. Franklin said. "He knows me well. You may take the letter with you. I'm sure he will make you most welcome."

Robert could hardly believe his good luck. During the following months, he saved all the money he could. He might be away for a long time. He wanted to be sure his mother was well taken care of while he was gone.

Robert worked harder than he had ever worked before. Then suddenly he became very ill. The doctor told him that he must go away from the city for a rest. If not, he might never get well again. So Robert went to a health resort for a vacation.

As the weeks passed, Robert began to feel better. He did not want to put off his trip any longer. He took most of his savings and bought his mother a small farm. Now she would have a place of her own, no matter what happened to him.

Surely, Robert thought, he would feel better soon. And surely he would be able to earn a little money in London to live on.

As his sailing ship moved silently out of the harbor, 21-year-old Robert took a last look at America. Safe in his pocket was Mr. Franklin's letter to Mr. West. Filled with new hopes and new dreams, Robert looked forward to the days ahead.

Chapter 7

Artist and Inventor

The trip across the Atlantic was long. But the rest and the sea air made Robert feel better. He was glad, though, when the voyage was over.

His heart was beating fast with excitement when he arrived at Mr. West's house in London.

Mr. West read Mr. Franklin's letter. Then he asked about Robert's work in Philadelphia, his family and friends. He said he would be happy to have Robert as one of his students.

"Until you find a place to live, you

must stay with my wife and me," he added.

As the months passed, Robert found that there was much to learn. In one letter to his mother he wrote: "Painting requires more study than I at first imagined."

The months became a year. He continued to study for another four years. During this time Robert was able to sell only a few of his paintings. Sometimes he became very discouraged.

After five years, he felt he had been a student long enough.

"I should be earning a living by painting," Robert said to Mr. West one day. "If only the Royal Academy would accept some of my paintings! Then people would buy my pictures."

Mr. West agreed with Robert. The academy was very important in England.

Paintings of only the best artists were shown there. Mr. West was a leading member of the academy.

Not long after this, Mr. West brought Robert some good news. "The academy has agreed to show two of your paintings," he said.

"That is wonderful!" Robert said.

"Yes, it is a great honor." Then Mr. West frowned. "As your friend, Robert, I must speak the truth. You will be a good artist, but I do not think you will ever be a great one."

Robert felt sad. He had tried to do his best for such a long time. "If you say so, I believe you, sir," Robert said at last. "If I cannot be a great artist, I do not want to be an artist at all."

"What will you do?" Mr. West asked.

"I don't want to go back to America yet," Robert answered. "I will look for a new opportunity here first. I will paint until I find other work."

Shortly after this, Robert met the duke of Bridgewater. The wealthy duke planned to build small canals throughout England. But there were problems to be solved. New ways to build canals were needed to make his plan work.

After talking with the duke, Robert began to think about these problems. "Perhaps," he said excitedly, "I could invent new machines to help build the canals."

Eagerly he read everything he could find about canals. Then he hurried off to the city of Birmingham, in central England. Here a few new canals were being built.

He watched the workmen dig the canals. The work went slowly because everything had to be done by hand.

Then he talked with the men who had planned the canals.

This trip gave him some new ideas. By 1794 he had invented several machines. One solved the problem of moving boats through the canals. The other was a machine that could be used to dig the canals.

Everywhere Robert looked he found a need for inventions. Sometimes his friends gave him ideas too. One friend, the earl of Stanhope, was also an inventor. He was very interested in steamboats.

"Could a steam engine be used to run a boat?" he asked Robert.

"I'm sure it could," Robert said. "A number of men have tried to build steamboats. Yet for one reason or another they have all failed. I have a plan for one that I think would work."

He drew a picture of what his boat would look like and gave it to Lord Stanhope. Someday, he hoped, he would have the time and money needed to build a steamboat.

By 1796 Robert had given up painting. Now he was able to earn a living as an inventor. He had several new ideas for inventions he wanted to work on.

Then one day an American friend brought him some bad news.

"English ships have attacked our American ships again," his friend said. "With France and England at war, no ships are safe from attack."

"The seas should be safe for all," Robert said angrily.

"England wants to rule the seas," his friend said. "The fighting won't stop until the British navy is beaten."

Suddenly Robert had a thought. "I will invent a terrible war machine," he told his friend. "After it is used once, no country will dare use it again. It will put an end to war forever."

"Then you should start to work on it at once, Robert," his friend said. "Unless peace comes soon, America may be forced into the war too."

"France must stop the British before this happens," Robert said. "And she will need my new invention to do so. I will go to Paris as soon as possible. I am sure I can raise the money there to build my war machine."

Chapter *8*

The Diving Boat

Robert went to Paris in 1797. There he met Joel Barlow and his wife. They were also Americans. Mr. Barlow was a diplomat. He worked for the American government in France.

The Barlows liked Robert very much. They asked him many questions about himself and his inventions.

"I want to sell my inventions for canals to the French," he answered. "That would give me enough money to build my war machine."

As Robert talked, he quickly drew a picture of it. He showed it to the Barlows.

"This is what it looks like—an underwater bomb and a diving boat," he told them. "I call the bomb a torpedo, and the boat a submarine. Because the boat can travel underwater, it cannot been seen or heard. It can silently carry the torpedo close to an enemy ship for a surprise attack."

"It's a daring idea, Robert." Mr. Barlow looked at Robert's drawing with interest. "I've never heard of a diving boat—or submarine—before."

"Perhaps you've forgotten, sir," Robert said. "One was built in America in 1776 by David Bushnell. It failed. It could travel only a short distance underwater. I must make my submarine much better."

"I like your idea, Robert," Mr. Barlow said. "France could use your war machine to stop the British. I will do what I can to help you."

"I will help you, too, to meet some nice young ladies," Mrs. Barlow added. "You must not work all the time."

Robert smiled. "I will be glad for your help, madam." He thanked Mr. Barlow. He was happy that he had found such good friends.

Through the Barlows, Robert met many important people in France. But the French had little time to think about building canals. The war was going badly for them. Their navy was weak, and the English were winning.

However, with the Barlows' help, Robert found money to build the torpedo. But when he tested it, it did not work right. Now he needed more money, so that he could build another one.

Several times he asked the French government to help him. He hoped to get enough money to build the submarine as well as a new torpedo. But each time the government said no.

Then in 1799 he had sad news from America. His mother had died. How he wished he could have seen her once more!

As Robert thought of his mother, he remembered her words: "Your head is full of good ideas, Robert." He knew she would not want him to give up.

"Somehow I will find a way to earn the money I need," he told Mr. Barlow. "I will pay for the submarine and torpedo myself. Then I will prove they work."

To earn money he decided to paint a few portraits. Then he painted a huge picture called a panorama. Nothing like it had ever been seen before in Paris. People paid to see it. By early 1800 Robert had enough money to build the submarine.

He and his helpers started to work on it in a little shop near the Seine River. It was to be built of wood and would measure 20 feet long. When the boat was finished, Robert named it the *Nautilus.*

In July people lined the banks of the river to see the strange boat. The Barlows and some men from the French government were there too. They watched as Robert and his two helpers climbed aboard.

"Good luck!" Mr. Barlow called to Robert.

"Do be careful, Robert," Mrs. Barlow added.

Robert smiled and waved to his friends. Then he and his men went down inside the boat.

Robert made sure everything was shut tight, so that no water could leak in. His helpers started turning the cranks. These were fastened to the boat's propellers. The *Nautilus* began to move.

When the boat reached the deeper waters of the wide river, it stopped. Then to the amazement of the people, it slowly sank out of sight.

There were cries of alarm from many in the crowd. They wondered if Robert and his men were drowning.

"Are they all right, Joel?" Mrs. Barlow asked her husband. "Robert is taking such a terrible chance!"

"Robert is a smart young man," Mr. Barlow said calmly. "He knows what he is doing."

Eight minutes later, the submarine came into sight again. Then it dived once more. This time it stayed down much longer.

Robert was very pleased with the success of these tests. So were the men from the French government. They said he would be paid if his war machine could sink any British ships.

In the months that followed, Robert made a new kind of torpedo. This one was a success. He also tested the submarine again. Now he was ready to prove how well his war machine would work in battle.

In the summer of 1801 he set out to sink some British warships. They

were anchored near the French coast. Somehow the British learned of Robert's plan. Before he could attack, they sailed away to safety.

Robert knew his war machine would work, but he had lost the chance to prove it. For the time being, he would have to put it aside. He was already interested in an idea for another invention.

Chapter 9

Steamboat Wreck

Early in 1801 Robert had met the new United States minister to France, Robert Livingston. Mr. Livingston was a wealthy businessman, as well as a diplomat.

Mr. Livingston had told Robert he wanted to find an inventor who could build a steamboat. He planned to use it to carry passengers between New York City and Albany, New York.

It was 150 miles from one city to the other. The journey by coach over poor roads was very slow and tiring. Sailboats could move much faster up the Hudson River.

"But sailboats can't travel without wind," Robert said.

"That's why our country so badly needs steamboats," Mr. Livingston said. "Do you think you could build a practical steamboat, Robert?"

Robert had been interested in steamboats for a long time. "Yes, I believe I could," he said eagerly.

So in 1802 Robert and Mr. Livingston became business partners. Robert would plan and build a steamboat in France. Mr. Livingston would help pay for it. If this boat was a success, Robert would return to America to build a much larger boat. This boat would become the Hudson River passenger boat.

Robert drew plans for the steamboat. In the spring of 1803 he started to build it. He could not afford to buy a new steam engine, so he rented one. It was big and heavy, but he thought it would work for this first test.

At last, after many weeks of hard work, the boat was finished. Its wooden hull was 70 feet long and 8 feet wide. There was a large paddle wheel on each side of the boat.

Robert was very proud of his boat. In a few days he planned to test it. A large crowd would be there to watch.

After a last day of work, he made sure the boat was safely tied to its dock on the Seine River. Then he went home to bed.

Before dawn the next morning, he was suddenly awakened. The wind was

blowing hard, and rain was beating against the window. Someone was knocking loudly on his door.

"Mr. Fulton, come quickly," a man's voice called. "Your boat is sinking!"

Hurriedly Robert dressed and rushed to the dock. There in the shallow water he saw what was left of his boat. Wind and waves had banged it against the dock during the storm. The heavy engine had broken through the boat's bottom and had sunk.

Robert worked without stopping for the next 24 hours. He and his helpers pulled the engine out of the water. He was happy to find that the engine was not broken. But the wooden hull of the boat was badly damaged.

Robert was wet, tired, and sick from working so hard. He was angry too. He knew that he had made a big mistake. He should have built a stronger hull to carry the heavy steam engine. He was so discouraged that he felt like giving up.

Yet he did not want to let his partner and his friends down. They believed he could succeed where others had failed.

After a few days' rest, Robert went back to work. He and his workmen rebuilt the hull of the boat. This time they built a stronger one.

By August the new steamboat was ready for a test. On August 9, 1803, Robert and three helpers built a wood fire under the engine's boiler. Clouds of thick gray smoke rolled out of the smokestack.

In a little while the water in the boiler became hot enough to make steam. The steam made the engine go.

And the engine worked the paddle wheels. Slowly they began to turn.

Many important people had been invited to watch the test. For several hours Robert steered the steamboat slowly up and down the river. Everyone saw that Robert's boat was a success.

To Robert this was just the beginning. He knew the Hudson River boat would need to be almost twice as big as this steamboat. There must be plenty of space for many passengers. Its engine would have to be strong enough to turn its giant paddle wheels. Yet it could not be too big or heavy.

"There is only one company in the world that can make the engine I need," he told Mr. Livingston. "That is James Watt's company, Boulton & Watt, in England."

"Very well then," Mr. Livingston said. "Order the engine from them."

Robert wrote the letter at once. Then he waited and waited.

It took three long years to get the engine. There was one delay after another. This made Robert angry and impatient. But there was nothing he could do to speed the engine on its way.

At last, in 1806, it was shipped to America. In October of that year Robert, too, sailed for home.

Chapter *10*

The Hudson River Steamboat

Robert's return to America was a happy one. His name had become well known. Many people had heard of his work with the steamboat in France. Government leaders had heard of his other inventions too.

Shortly after Robert's return home, President Thomas Jefferson asked him to help build an important canal. Robert was sorry to say no, but he was already planning the Hudson River steamboat.

When the plans were finished, he took them to Charles Brown, a shipbuilder. Mr. Brown's shipyard was near New York City.

Robert visited it often. He watched carefully as workmen built the boat's huge hull. It was twice as big as Robert's first steamboat.

When it was finished the hull was towed to Robert's workshop on the Hudson River. Here he had been making small changes in the engine and the boiler. Robert knew that it was important for the engine, boiler, and paddle wheels to work perfectly together.

One day he and his workmen carefully lowered the engine into place. They put it inside the hull near the center of the boat. The boiler and its smokestack were lowered into place behind the engine. At last the huge paddle wheels were put on the outside of the hull.

A workman shook his head. "Looks like it's half barge and half ship," he said to another workman. "I don't think it will ever work."

Many people were curious about this funny-looking boat. They came down to see it. They joked about it. Most of them had never seen a steam engine before. They thought Robert was foolish to put one in a boat. They called the boat "Fulton's Folly."

Robert and his partner named the steamboat the *Clermont*. This was the name of Mr. Livingston's home that overlooked the Hudson River.

Robert and Mr. Livingston invited about 40 friends to be the *Clermont*'s first passengers. Among them was one

of Mr. Livingston's relatives, Harriet Livingston.

Robert had met her when he first returned to America. Soon he had fallen in love with her. He was very happy to have her with him on this voyage.

On August 17, 1807, the *Clermont* began its trip to Albany. The dock and nearby shore were crowded with people. They laughed and shouted at Robert. But he paid no attention to the noisy crowd. He stood proudly on deck as the *Clermont* steamed away from the dock.

Robert returned to New York on the *Clermont* a few days later. The first trip on his steamboat had been a great success. The passengers had had a fast, safe, comfortable journey.

Robert was glad that people liked his

steamboat. He was glad for another reason too. He and Harriet were going to be married soon.

In September the steamboat was renamed the *North River*. It began to make regular trips between New York and Albany. Each week more and more people traveled on it.

Within the next few years Robert had several more steamboats built. Some ran as ferryboats to Brooklyn and New Jersey.

Another steamboat, the *New Orleans*, was planned by Robert. It was built in Pittsburgh by Nicholas Roosevelt. It was the first steamboat to travel down the Ohio and Mississippi rivers. This voyage was made by Mr. Roosevelt in 1811.

These were busy years for Robert. He was now the father of four small children—one son and three daughters. His home was a happy, noisy place. And he was working harder than ever.

He wanted to build steamboats to be used in India and Russia. The United States government asked him to help plan the great Erie Canal. He had already done more work on the submarine and torpedo.

He had also drawn plans for the world's first steam-powered battleship. The United States government started building it in 1814. In honor of Robert, it was named *Fulton the First*.

Robert did not live to see the battleship or his many other plans completed. In January 1815 he became ill. On February 23, 1815, he died at his home in New York City.

People everywhere were sorry to hear of Robert's death. His family and friends remembered his kind, gentle ways. His workmen remembered his great skill as a mechanic. Young artists and inventors remembered the help he had given them.

Many government leaders honored him for his work. "Robert Fulton gave us the first practical steamboat," said one. "Other inventors did pioneering work that helped him. But Fulton was the one who made the steamboat work."

"Yes," said another, "and he shared his inventions with many countries. The whole world will miss Robert Fulton."